Those Who Can't Do

by Katherine Finstuen

with illustrations by
Jessica Lyman Finstuen

Those Who Can't Do

Copyright © 2022 by Katherine Finstuen
Published by Waterton Publishing Company
Crystal River Books
watertonpublishing.com
ISBN 978-1-7347632-5-6

All rights reserved. No part of this book may be reproduced, stored, or transmitted by any means whether auditory, graphic, mechanical, or electronic without written permission of the author, except in the case of brief excerpts used in critical articles and reviews. Unauthorized reproduction of any part of this work is illegal and is punishable by law.

Because of the dynamic nature of the Internet, any web addresses or links contained in this book may have changed since publication and may no longer be valid. The views expressed in this work are solely those of the author and do not necessarily reflect the views of the publisher, and the publisher hereby disclaims any responsibility for them.

For My Parents

Prologue

In some odd recipe of the mind, two books, read years apart, have sifted their ingredients, dividing my thought batches in certain, perhaps alarming, configurations. In Anne Lamott's *Bird by Bird: Some Instructions on Writing and Life*, she recounts her father's guidance regarding a long-neglected science project. Her brother, faced with this seemingly insurmountable task, was advised "Bird by bird, buddy. Just take it bird by bird." She applies this approach to writing. Just as she taught me a system for composition, Matt Sewell's *A Charm of Goldfinches* instructed me in the enchanting world of ornithological terminology. Having long embraced a tenderness for the collective noun, I decided upon a task that would involve grouping my own word birds in a rather different manner. My version of these various flocks which swoop through the mind trace their intricate patterns below, bird by (tortured) bird.

Logue

A Pestilence of Pygmy Nuthatches

Fifteen years, seven principals, two talkings-to. Yes, those figures are accurate. The first time a principal received a complaint meriting a visit, I was accused of harassing a business in a neighboring town. The second time involved my propensity for sitting in a large cardboard box at times during class. There was no harassment involved, but yes the box accusation was true. The added information the parent supplied — that the teacher in question (me) suffered from a disorder causing her to hide from her students in said box — now that was entirely inaccurate. I suppose some context is called for.

It's difficult being an English teacher out there in the wild. It's not as if I know every grammar rule; the different tenses of lie and lay will forever mystify me, and my childhood education lacked any form of structured language lessons. Diagram a sentence? What's that? But I truly believe we can all handle the use of apostrophes for contractions and for possession, not plurals. I also trust we can grasp the difference between "everyday" and "every day." Based on walks, visits to businesses, and viewings of signs, these convictions are proven wrong on a daily basis. In my classroom, I dedicated one section as the Wall of Shame; students could display pictures of blundered grammar and misspelled signs. I tacked up several of my own, including part of a yogurt cup reading "Use everyday for" with a list of suggestions (as if we couldn't figure that one out)** and a picture of a store selling costumes and decorations called "Lets Party." No apostrophe. Willing students could take part in the mission to correct these grave offenses. I instructed them to be polite but forthright, to call or write the two businesses. Many joined my cause. The owner of "Lets Party" was not amused. Principal #2 bade me cease and desist and I caved. Deeming the employed state of being the favorable one at the time, I dared not channel my inner Patrick Henry: "Give me proper punctuation or give me death!" So years have passed and still the sign blares its garish mistake.

The store sits adjacent a gas station. I recall one afternoon as I filled the tank and fumed, wondering if a ladder and a can of paint could abet me in some strategically placed graffiti editing during a future dead of night. I then noticed a police car pulling into the pump ahead of me. It took all my willpower not to approach the officer and proclaim, "Sir, I'd like to report a missing apostrophe."

Principal #6 visited regarding the box grievance. Though on my side and considering the call absurd, the slander still smarted. Here I'm wondering if I need to request that you suspend your disbelief, although perhaps you, too, know the unique spell cast by the oversized cardboard box and no suspension bridge over the skeptical depths need be constructed. My love of such encasements originated in childhood. My best friend's parents bought a new refrigerator; we inherited a castle. My neighbors purchased a new washing machine; a make believe caboose scooted into our backyard. This enchantment may have embered but did not extinguish entirely. One morning on visiting the staff room, I spied a post-delivery stack of recyclables; immediately a thought bubble visible to those with any discernible imagination skimmed over my head. "I want to get *in* that." Following an awkward, encumbered walk back to the classroom, I deposited my treasure, one boxy lady.

So yes, when mood struck, I'd enter the box and teach from there — an odd dais, perhaps, but one seemingly enjoyed by all concerned (meaning me, though I believe my audience appreciated the innovation). Over the summer, thinking it was trash (??!!!), the custodial staff removed and presumably destroyed my beloved abode. I remained boxless for months and then, when a junior girl asked what her mom could do to repay my favor (I'd ridiculously agreed to edit her mother's college paper), I considered, and then replied, "I'd like another big box." Boom. The fun continued...until that call.

Other people ruin everything.

When I told my colleagues the story (and they, understanding either the pleasure of giant bits of cardboard fastened together or just my quirky amusements) assumed dismayment on my behalf. They also taught me, and how I never learned of this slang previously I know not, that "box" happens to be a slang term for a certain part of the female anatomy, so of course we've had fun with the fact that the principal had to talk to me about my box, that he defended it, that I offered to get rid of it because hey — I wasn't using it all that much. This led my department chair to tell me about something on FaceBook that comes to her every few months — an instruction to name one's vagina based on the last movie the individual has watched. I asked if a series would be permissible and she said yes. *Lady Dynamite* she is. I told my mother the whole story before inquiring about her latest movie: *Florence Foster Jenkins*. Of course.

Not that I'm going to start naming my vagina, but I am glad I hadn't just watched *The Big Lebowski* or *Finding Neverland*.

**After much persistence and struggle, the yogurt company edited its error-ridden container, though still preserving its list of helpful possibilities for the lacto-uninspired.

A Demise of Roosters

Is it a wonder I want to quit my job? The problem: money. Thus I've decided to pursue a few ideas guaranteed to pad my bank account, allowing me to live the sort of idle life I desire.

First I will develop a new antisocial media program. The only available feature involves posting a blank screen. This function can be accessed at most once a day. What will it be called? In deference to those odd (and paradoxical) sheets of paper included in certain business mailings: This Page Intentionally Left Blank (TPILB for the acronym-prone). The motto: "You are not a product. Stop treating yourself as one." I want people to stop advertising themselves. It *will* take off. I'm hoping in a positive way, but given humans, I'm sure it'll somehow morph into yet another status barometer. Just how much are you *not* showing off? I do not know how that will be measured but again, given humans I'm sure we'll find a way. But by that time I'll have made a pile, so who cares? Well I do — I don't want my creation pulling a Frankenstein's creature on me. I'm in a fantasy here already, so why not make it an optimistic one for a few moments, a few words? People will remain on TPILB for as long as they need that posting fix, but eventually they won't need even that. Maybe they'll start talking again, connecting again, leaving that record of mind munching artificiality buried deep within their devices' histories.

Another will prove the new sensation of the bakery world. It seems that the cupcake craze, the crepe frenzy, the oat ball perversity have reached a yeasty peak and are being punched down by the mighty hand (and wandering mouth) of the consumer. Inspiration hit — if that's the correct term for such an idea steeped in a murky tea of bleakness — when I once again drove by a series of flags across town waving their sorrowful message halfway down their respective poles. "Why not make that their permanent place?" I wondered. They're up and down like candy-cluttered kids on pogo sticks. Who can keep up? And besides, tragedy is more of the state of our union than anything else. Let us accept this sorry fact and allow our emblem to more accurately reflect the real state of this disunion. Therefore I am marketing toothpick-ridden flags at half pick. Stick them in your red, white, and blue 4th of July cupcakes, let them banner your eclair, declaim from your pie, whether All-American apple or no, gloomily celebrate from the frosted whorls atop your birthday cake. Let our sweet treats speak truth even as we add to the girthy and diabetes-infused waistlines of yes, our real America.

And finally, allow me to introduce my most brilliant scheme: the sheet set with a fully fitted bottom sheet, half fitted top sheet, and the standard pillowcase (or cases depending upon the amount of fluffdom crowning your bed). But damnit, someone told me this ingenuity already exists. Just where, though? I've never seen them. I've never been able to make such an easy bed to lie in.

Should my inventions fail to succeed, what else can I do... this one so lovingly classified among those who *can't* do? Sometimes I imagine becoming a professional noticer of people — a state subsidized job in that I boost the well-being of its citizens (still in froth-topped fantasyland here!). It is vital to know one's strengths. I'm good at noticing people, at remembering details about their lives. People long to be seen. Why else would social media prove such an addiction to so many? Perhaps if more real-life noticers existed, no weaning off through the magic of TPILB would prove necessary. Barring this career, please just send me your signs and containers before construction or manufacture. I'll make sure your apostrophes are in the right place, that the sumptuous items listed on the dessert menu include peach cobbler, not peach clobber, that your exercise class is advertised correctly — as cardio kickboxing rather than dickboxing. This I *can* do.

A Cruel and Unusual Punishment of Geese

Many people speak of themselves as being forgetful, but does anyone pride themselves on being rememberful? I've never heard it and only said it myself for the first time today. At 42. Granted, it's not a word. But why isn't it a word? Because it isn't an accurate description of the human race? Well, we do probably forget a lot more than we remember but there are people with spectacular memories — whether because they're some sort of savant, addicted to spite, or else incredibly thoughtful. And it's not as if there aren't words for plenty of obscure things. Just as "rememberful" should make its way into the language, other terms have worked for us long enough and must be forced, if necessary, into retirement.

While I admit I haven't read it (it's quite the tome) the title speaks to my heart: *The War Against Cliche*. It rests, unread, on my shelves but it pleases me to know that someone else shares a similar loathing. Now I'm tempted to use one myself. My misery here does indeed love some company, even if it comes in the form of Martin Amis. Oh but I am tired of the stale language used by so many. More acceptable in conversation, of course, but in professional writing? Sometimes I wonder at the author's mental stability, not to mention their editor's, for letting such phrases as "hit the nail on the head" or "sharp as a tack," or "through thick and thin" pass into permanent copy. The not only uninteresting, but confounding "turned on his/her heel" (who, honestly, does that?) needs to be kicked not to the curb, but past the goal post and subsequently explode due to its being shoddily made in a Sri Lankan sweat factory. Original language gives me a thrill, whereas this pap churns in me a desire to hibernate, even if it means sharing a den with half-starved bears. There are certain expressions I never again wish to encounter. If I read yet another description of a woman clicking across the floor in staccato heels, I might grab one of those heels and, Oedipus-like, gouge out my eyes so those reprehensible pages are no longer visible. Nor do I want to see the phrase "despite or perhaps because of." Please just stop. Not quite a cliche but it's a description that pains me to the core: Can reviewers of books binding a scant number of pages cease referring to them as "slim volumes"? There are other ways to describe diminutive texts.

There is one cliche I do love and desire to inhabit myself: the ineffectual secretary. I ache to play this part — several times over — in the movies. To be typecast as her. Not ineffectual as in messing up phone messages, copies, document formatting, but hopeless at keeping unwelcome visitors from entering the main office. "You can't go in there!" proclaimed in a determined voice, only to be unceremoniously pushed aside. A look of surprised wonder slathered over my features like butter on a biscuit. Make-up and padding, or lack thereof, could morph me into any number of powerless amanuenses. Of the myriad casting directors now reading these words, consider this my application.

A Waterboarding of Skylarks

The levels of misunderstandings are vast. Let us imagine them as floors in a many-storied building. No, I do not wish to push the button for Level 15, "Irreparable Damage to a Relationship" and Level 2 "Playful Mishearing of Words" can be a fun diversion, but where I want those sliding doors to open, allowing me to alight and roam, is Level 8 "Wild Inaccuracies Eventually Leading to Overwhelming Mirth." Wasn't that Edith Wharton's working title for the miserable adventures of Lily Bart? There are many occupied rooms on this floor, but the one I most enjoy frequenting involves my fake parental status and subsequent mind travel of a friendly neighbor. Where to even begin, though? Perhaps with my aversion to parenthood itself.

While I adore moms and find what they do and are capable of feeling one of the most magnificent examples of human behavior, I have never longed to be one. Maybe because I have no intense natural liking for children and harbor downright indifference toward babies. This, combined with a certainty that I would not shine as a mother myself (I'm far too selfish and addicted to my own needs and wants), it's never been a consideration.

Yet one day in my late 30s, an encounter with my TA of the year left me with an immaculately conceived, nearly adult child. I profess to being rather feminine in outward appearance and on the far end of the heterosexual side of the spectrum, not that I've had much luck on that end of the horizon. I'm like a boxer who gets knocked out again and again, taking longer to return the ring after each emotional beating. In fact, I've pretty much hung up my gloves, which I suppose could be a euphemism for celibacy — no condoms necessary. Not only was I surprised by the dear girl's confession on that mild spring morning (although we had grown close and developed a wonderful connection), but also by the role she'd assigned me in her life.

"You've become a father to me," she said.

Okay then. I took her to her first baseball game, after she departed for college I'd see her on breaks for little outings, we exchanged cards and emails. Eventually I bequeathed my box to her, which she transformed into a terrarium for her bearded dragon (so yes, my box is now inhabited by a large lizard — make of that what you will). What a glorious way to become a parent, I mused. No pregnancy, no birth, largely through the teenage years, and she's happily ensconced in an institution of higher learning, the tuition for which is forked over by her real parents.

At times my faux parentage would come up with friends and neighbors and they would later inquire about my kids (my daughter's twin eventually adopted herself into the family). I received Father's Day cards from them and, although our meetings grew fewer, the trio continued; we were family after all.

Last spring the Muddle approached, sniffing about for a place to curl up. On Mother's Day I received a sweet message from a neighbor I'd grown acquainted with but in my response I did remind him I was the father, not the mother, of twins. I did not hear back. This did not fluster even though Richard's typical behavior favored immediate response. The days passed and then there appeared the following confusing note: "I'm honored you chose to confide in me. It clarifies some things you mentioned in the past...I can't even imagine how upsetting your journey has been."

I've never liked being filmed, but I'll confess a longing that a camera recorded my face through its phases of understanding: bafflement while writing back, perplexed reflection after hitting send, the sudden dawning of clarity regarding his belief: I used to be a man. I want to observe the knowledge of his misconception ripple over my features. I later attempted a gentle but clarifying note of my own regarding the lifelong consistency of my sex.

The episode attained a higher degree of satisfaction with his follow-up explanation, misspellings and all — the process by which he cobbled the "truth" of the matter together. I'll admit by this time I'd forgotten a long ago chance encounter in the waiting room of an out of town endocrinology clinic. At the time I'd found it an interesting coincidence, but this occurrence played as one more piece of the sex change puzzle of my identity. "Ok. I'm glad we got that cleared up. Blame the whole miss understanding on [your kid]. Hope your not laughing on the floor at me. When you said that I thought of the endocrinology appointment…Extrapolated a bit to far there. Red in the face here."

Oh Richard, all I feel for you and that blushing visage is gratitude for compelling the finger of my imaginary elevator operator (a profession I can scarcely believe ever existed) to select Level 8 with such delicious frequency.

An Unlawful Search and Seizure of Wrens

I'm sure we've all had them, though they differ from individual to individual. No, not cases of chickenpox, but childhood fascinations. When I think back, a number of such curiosities surface and sparkle but one of great significance involves double scoops of ice cream. Perhaps its magic is woven into context — our yearly family summer lake vacation — in itself a sanctuary of water and sun, towels drying over fences like the flags of colorful and exotic countries, the entirety slathered in coconutty lotion. Still I believe if I'd encountered such a dessert on just one fortuitous occasion rather than part of a treasured tradition, the sweet perfection of creativity would remain securely locked in my vault of wonders. We always stopped at the same small town on our journey for a bathroom, stretch, and food break. The kids never varied in their destination — a sweet shop/ ice cream parlor right in the town center, nor did my mother deviate from her path to its neighboring bakery — both destinations of sugared ornate opulence, divine in both visual and olfactory sensations. She'd select an apricot Danish from all the creamed and frosted intricacies of the display case, then usher us to the altar of ice cream. Our choices sometimes involved the purely (to me now) disgusting: bubblegum. What was I thinking? But we were always allowed to choose two flavors. What differed in this establishment were the cones holding our orders. Instead of the usual cones with one scoop riding atop the other, it contained two platforms, the scoops cozily adjacent, as if nestling upon an edible loveseat. Who had thought of this ingenious arrangement? Why did it not catch on, available in all the shops (and shoppes) the country round? Yet, I have never encountered such again.

And was my path toward a career in frozen dairy desserts paved with them? Not that it's my trade now, but Baskin-Robbins sowed the first seeds on the barren field of my resume. There I scooped, made sundaes, shakes, the innovative Cappuccino Blast and all its variants, stocked, spent an extra restorative few moments in the walk-in freezer on the very hottest days of the Spokane summer, huddled near the ice cream cases (the heating elements in their lower half a gift during the slow, snow-muffled days in winter). At the end of the night I mopped and wiped down the sides of the ice cream vats so they shone pristine and pretty instead of smeared and dirty — the smearing transfering to myself; I always arrived home with forearms covered in a sticky brown, a temporary case of vitiligo. I worked other jobs too — a paper and gift store, a deli, Starbucks, used books, and finally, the last of this ilk before I began teaching, a gig at a self-serve frozen yogurt shop (an establishment where I was asked not once, but multiple times, "Is fat free less fat than nonfat?" It turns out there *are* stupid questions). All these jobs paid a negligible wage and, though there were downsides to each, they all rank higher than my experience as a high school teacher. Maybe it's the level of stress, my inability to shed its mind torments after hours, the truly whacked parents. Not to say the customers were perfect by any means. I particularly remember yes, fully grown adults throwing near tantrums if we happened to be out of their favorite toppings. I took to placing little notes on the empty bins when such life-altering catastrophes befell: "Yes, we *are* out of strawberries, but you *will* be okay." Even so, I there experienced the glory of attacking Oreos and Butterfinger bars with a rubber-topped mallet, a performance of such release and restoration it should be offered as therapeutic treatment in spas everywhere.

Apart from genuinely enjoying the majority of my tasks, I'm grateful for experiencing life on the other side of the counter. I feel I would always have been polite to grocery store clerks, those in charge of flight check-in, ticket takers, waiters, waitresses, garage attendants and the like, but my own time spent in places just like theirs has me acknowledging the humanity and unique mystery of their existence. I say mystery because — not an original thought — can we ever truly understand each other? During my tenure at Baskin-Robbins, I played a game with myself. While waiting for the customers to place their orders, I attempted guessing what that order would entail. Not once did I predict correctly. I worked there long enough to develop a scooping callus on my right palm (I named her Belinda), but not long enough to comprehend the hidden depths of others.

I do recall desperately wishing a patron would someday request a double scoop — vanilla paired with French vanilla. Months passed and the yearned for purchase manifested. After the young man paid and departed, licking his abundance of varying vanillas, my soul effervesced. I later learned my best friend bribed him into realizing this double-dipped dream.

A Solitary Confinement of Lovebirds

Yesterday afternoon found me enveloped in birdsong, delicate meadowflower, grasses wind-rippling the hills. The sun coaxed my long-sleeved tee from shoulders to a subtle waist hug, the temperature and the softest of breezes kissed my skin — every inch. Walking accompanied by keyring alone has attuned me to the variants of breezes, from soft exhalations to balance-challenging gales. On all but the stillest days there's a music on the trails, the forest soundtrack a balm for the constant barrage of human voices, grumbling motors, computer tones. Right up there with litterers and grocery cart abandoners (who, if I believed in hell and there existed any such circular organization as Dante divined, would find a filing space for themselves in one of the lower circles) exist fellow walkers and joggers inflicting their own selections on others due to sheer volume or absence of earbuds. There's a reason I choose to stride unplugged. Spare me the tinny reproductions of your music or podcast. And if you simply must be so inconsiderate, at least don't have crappy taste.

Although perhaps the two are concomitant?

We are far too scared of silence these days, of subtle tones. This new trend of city promenades and squares piping in music is one I wish extinct. There are too many of us with differing tastes to please us all and if you've ever been forced to sit through a loathed selection while trying to find repose in a public space, you know the torture of such an experience. I'm thinking of changing dentists, come to think of it. My forced immobility there has too often been paired with the awfulness of country mewling or soft rock insipidity that loyalty and a capable doctor pale.

But why scared? It reminds me of a time when a colleague, attempting a mini-lesson on the American transcendentalists, asked her students to spread out in the woods behind the classroom sans backpacks, sans phones, sans anything. The assignment: sit silently for five minutes. When she finished explaining, Jimmy wailed, "Oh no! Don't leave me alone with my thoughts!"

Yes, our minds can be frightening places — haunted houses filled with innumerable thought pattern hamster wheels, booby trap explosions of craziness — but cheerful places — hilarity, love, kindness, and joy can and do exist just down the street. One block over a complex of anxiety, restlessness, shame, and stress, but across the park a duplex where peace resides in whose cozy compartments dwell memories that soothe.

Allow me space, silence, and time for reflection. *Do* leave me alone with my thoughts. I can then close my eyes, tapping lightly on that first door. Entering, I revisit my mother as she makes the bed, myself among the linens. Bottom sheet embracing the mattress and pillows pocketed in cases, I lie back and watch the top sheet fall in soft grace (admittedly, my half-fitted sheet idea wouldn't partner well here) over and down the body, the snuggery of being freshly, tightly tucked in, the final heaviness of the top blanket and quilt. I cannot conceive of a better kiss goodnight, a finer wish for sweet dreams. Next door a similar sensation. On certain rainy days — a frequent occurrence in the Pacific Northwest of my childhood — the P.E. teacher unfurls the parachute. My classmates and I circle the chute, gripping it in tiny tight fists, one after the other, lift with all our tender strength, quickly scoot forward, and bring the material down behind us to sit on its edge. For a few magic-infused moments we sit in this darkened circle, the cloth dome mighty above our heads until its slow collapse around us. These two memories have formed a beautiful partnership within, two scoops on that double-sided cone so cherished. Something about soft billowing above, the sense of deep security and serenity...even if only enduring a precious few moments before melting me home to reality.

A Decapitation of Finches

Although teaching amply heaps life's grocery basket with miseries, it also provides the occasional delight. One of my first experiences involving such classroom joy arrived in the form of a drawing. While reading selections from *The Odyssey* with my 9th graders, I decided to have them choose a scene from the tale and illustrate it. "You won't be graded on your drawing ability — just try."

They seemed to enjoy this opportunity to evade reading and writing. Over time I've often witnessed the pleasure even teenagers find in wielding crayons and markers — of the latter, I always buy the odorless kind so don't assume they're simply enjoying the high. Somehow coloring has not lost its charm, even among the most apathetic and disengaged.

I collected their work to find a poster depicting Odysseus's escape from the Cyclops. By securing themselves beneath Cyclops's fleecy flock, the men freed themselves from the cave's odious confines. Ali chose to draw just one of these sheep with two backs. Never before had the flight plan struck me as untoward; never again will it strike me as toward. I maintain she didn't mean anything by it (or did she? — did she? — sweet little dumpling-souled Ali?). Whether intentional or no, this portrayal of seeming bestiality would not be among those chosen to grace the classroom wall. Though being me, of course I was tempted. I visualized myself before a roomful of parents on Back to School Night, directing attention to their children's most recent endeavors: "And here you will observe an odyssey of a different sort...our hero unsheathing his own Cyclops to plow the depths of ovine adventure. I believe the artist calls it *Fuck Ewe*." Oh the brazen beauty of dreams!

Here I evict my mind from the gutter and place a different part of my body elsewhere, the toilet bowl. Recalling another activity I've assigned — students are asked to think of things, types of people, or actions for which there are no words but ought to be. I've always thought, for example, there must be a specific noun for that globby accumulation on a bottle of lotion or shampoo, or a verb to express the indecent amount of said lotion or shampoo issuing from the container upon dislodgment of this obstruction. Not to mention the shame in the dearth of synonyms for the word thesaurus…

In this vein, I concocted a term and emailed it to my family with the following subject line: "new word with (sadly) autobiographical implications."

defenescate (v.) — the act of throwing one's excrement out the window (especially when experiencing plumbing issues in another's home that *may* lead to greater embarrassment than the act of defenescating itself)

I've never been one for scatological humor, but to me this isn't humorous. With age I've learned not to take the experience with which my body voids itself as an assurance, but to cherish and give thanks for reliable evacuation. Perhaps if I now met with a clogged toilet in my brother's girlfriend's house where she lived with *her* two brothers I would not have felt my hand and the window my only recourse, but when faced with the quandary of the blocked up bowl in a younger incarnation, yes, I took the matter in my own hands and tossed my problem away, seemingly forever. Seemingly for, instead of remaining in the bushy thicket where it landed, some of it somehow (an animal? an intense gust?) ended up in the front walkway many hours later. Returning from our outing of the day and approaching the entrance to the house my brother inquired of an *almost* uninformed audience, "What *is* that? It looks like poop…it looks like *human* poop."

Did I confess? No. I played dumb, in my silence vowing never to air my secret as I had aired my excrement. Months later, I did break my oath (backyard, family gathering, an atmosphere of sharing misfortunes involving that which issues from our bodies), and out the story splattered. For who among us — I'm certain the numbers are few considering the amount we excrete and defecate, combined with the amount and variety of facilities we encounter in our lifetimes and the state of repair and disrepair of these commodes — has yet to find themselves in a less than savory bathroom situation? Certainly my family proved empathetic.

I've always appreciated Ramona Quimby's question regarding Mike Mulligan (he of that esteemed shovel). Post storytime she asked, disconcerting her teacher, how he went to the bathroom. So real, so *human* a wonderment, Ramona. Can we just admit that we have bodies that don't do beautiful things? Although, if one has ever experienced digestive-related blockage, the production of a big healthy movement — why, that can be beautiful too.

Had I been convinced of this on that long ago afternoon, perhaps defenescation could have been avoided — both the deed and the neologism describing it. This reminds me of a term one teenage boy concoted during the language invention exercise which shall forever reside in my memory. I remain grateful I didn't ask the students to illustrate their creations; some dictionaries boast pictures, after all. A depiction of procrasturbation (I have every faith in my reader's ascertaining its meaning) is a consummation devoutly to be missed.

A Mugging of Penguins

To adopt a modern term, I've "identified" as a cantankerous old man (named Mr. Crabapple) since the age of nine or so. Thus I find certain pleasures of mine improbable: holiday cartoon specials, Mr. Toad's Wild Ride, Halloween costumes. Being stingy, I tend toward the more creative rather than ornate get ups — save when they're funded by others. When I confessed, in my 30s, an enduring ambition to dress as Alice in Wonderland, my mother surprised me with the beautifully perfect attire. I spent several October 31sts in this guise — one year even experiencing the joy of standing in line behind The Mad Hatter at the local grocery store on my way home from school. In this serendipitous state, I failed to notice if sugarlumps and tea comprised his purchases. Then in the second year of my medical debacles I bade goodbye to my honey-hued waves and hello to a stubbled dome. Sadly, I sensed it was time to retire the blue dress and pinafore unless, that is (and yes, I was tempted), I wished to masquerade as Alice in the Pediatric Oncology Ward. Somehow I felt certain individuals might find such posing insensitive or poor of taste.

My favorite self-styled creation was inspired by the Trader Joe's parking lots in which I've been forced to gingerly maneuver my (compact! so small are the spaces) car. How many dings, dents, raised digits, and altercations have resulted from this poor planning, I've often wondered. So one year I donned all black, striped myself vertically with masking tape, and greeted All Hallow's Morn as a Trader Joe's parking space. No, nobody guessed my costume's intention, but once I enlightened them, their comprehension gave way to a more intimate connection. "I, too, have suffered such confines in the pursuit of peanut butter-filled pretzels" their expressions seemed to convey. I sent a photo of myself to a friend in Boston with the attendant message inquiring if she understood what I meant, or was it different in her neighborhood. She responded that she certainly could identify, adding, "This is something that unites us all."

As darkness consumed the sun's lingering light, I reflected upon the reaction of one of my colleagues. Upon learning my identity, she eyed me closely. "So...you're tiny and awkward."

"Yes," I responded, perhaps too quickly. Somehow, I surmised her assessment referred to more than just my outfit.

Stripping the tape from pants and sweatshirt, I approached the wastebasket, sticky streamers floating in my wake. Gazing into its depths, I realized something. "I could use this!" Instead of tossing the tape, I affixed it to the towel rod for future necessity.

Halloween was over and Mr. Crabapple resumed his familiar place in my squashed pumpkin heart.

A Death Sentence of Ducks

There is something lovely about marking the passage of seasons, about delighting in those specific qualities that define each month. I can not recall with certainty when I first became aware of the intense antipathy I feel toward out of season decorations, but once the realization arose, its roots embedded themselves deep within my being.

A trip north to visit my mother in Portland solidified these feelings. It was the first week of August, sultry and sunny. A malfunctioning coffee pot, one that had perked its last brew, sent us to a nearby kitchen store for a replacement. Finding one that suited her needs, we approached the cashier. On the counter beside the register, an orange and black display of pumpkins and cats predominated. This jarred my tank top and shorts clad self. Halloween was not yet a glimpse on the horizon of the year; why detract from the carefree afternoons of summer with knick knacky portents of late October? It felt wrong. Returning home from my visit, I was further disturbed by a box of pumpkin-shaped Snickers bars garishly presiding over the check-out stand of my local grocery store.

I must admit it's not only the early holiday interlopers that offend, but those refusing to disappear after the time for that particular celebration has expired. I became a crusader against such dated stragglers on a bright day in May. Weary of the pumpkins still settled snugly on my neighbors' porch, I reacted. With no one about, I grabbed them, hurling them in the dumpster. Some guilt was involved in this act, no doubt due to the destruction of property, so the next fall, as the leaves transformed and the light sharpened, I decided upon replacing them. As an afterthought I added three baby pumpkins to my purchase, for who knows what those mature pumpkins found themselves doing in their leisure months? One crisp evening, with only the moon and stars as witnesses, I positioned this gourdy family on that same porch. The following day I heard the wife exclaim in shock to her husband, "Charlie! The pumpkins are back!" In more recent years I've taken to carrying post-it notes with me. One bearing the message,

"This decoration is now an anachronism" I stuck to a potted poinsettia still lagging about on the Fourth of July. The Fourth of July!

Such behavior suggests a laziness or lack of that particular rigidity I am prone to, though I wonder if this inability to stay content within the seasons, in a now which will all too soon evaporate, relates to one of many nonsensical traits in humans. Perhaps that's my own foolery shining through — belief that our behaviors should make sense, but I've noticed certain propensities of ours contradicting their very goals. We are addicted to distraction and find being fully present in the moment both a rarity and incredibly difficult. To my mind these traits exhibit, if subconsciously, our collective reluctance to admit and accept our own demise. Yet, if we are constantly not being, then the big NOT BEING of our death shouldn't cause anxiety. If we could be one of those select few who do exist comfortably and without angst in the present, feeling themselves fully in it without that ceaseless desire for diversion, it would seem only those individuals should fear death, and yet the opposite appears to be the case. Which brings me to my favorite pencil. Not really. I just don't know what to make of this cosmic conundrum so would rather distract myself and others with fancies of an old, unused writing utensil. I say unused because if I use it, and thus cause necessary sharpening, its hilariousness will be destroyed. Now I feel I'm coming back to my original topic — my pencil exists right here, not dreaming of past writing excursions or looking toward future jottings. Or not. Maybe it's simply refusing to participate in life for participation will result in the ultimate cessation of it. Or it could be just a pencil that I, the agent, am forcing into suspended stasis for my own gratification. Stop it, mind. Just tell the impatient audience about this incredible find.

First I'll note my firm belief that whoever contrived said pencil didn't recognize the comic possibility inherent in its message. Nope. I think they just planned poorly and without imagination. I found it on the classroom floor, knowing at once it must be mine. Ostensibly it originally read "It's Not

Cool To Do Drugs!" but time and scribbling shortened its lesson. What had been a no doubt successful soldier in the war on drugs...yes, I'm being sarcastic here. Did the designer, at the moment of the idea's conception, imagine young Philip or Imogen reaching for a crack pipe from some pressuring peer (Tyler or Tiffany, those corrupting souls), and then notice, while erasing a misplaced apostrophe on their homework assignment (which they were diligently completing before accepting that danger-laden on ramp towards the highway [in ill repair] to the hell of addiction and subsequent whoredom leading nowhere but to the rocky bottom of a cliffside turn), stop and think "No, this pencil speaks truth. Its teaching is mightier than the pipe's!"?

Whatever. Its days of efficacy were over. I pocketed it, thus saving a generation from internalizing its new exhortation "Cool To Do Drugs!" Ahh, the virtue in hiding those words from impressionable teens. Drugs might lead to death, but then life leads to death, a subject we are all desperately trying to avoid. So we giddyup, reboarding that mad merry-go-round of not being while being. Like I said, it's a conundrum, one forcing me to admit my own hypocrisy.

While judgmental of the a-seasonal, I am clearly no stranger to mind maneuverings myself. Yet as challenging as staying in the moment can be, can we at least attempt to gain freedom from those thieves of time and savored sensations, achieving, if only temporarily, a sense of peace with the present, a present which shall pass all too soon?

Ghost cutouts and cobwebbed bushes trying to spook the dripping Popsicle from my sunkissed fist saps that distinctive cherry flavor; bright red and green schematics take me away from the enjoyments and pleasure of the vibrant oranges and yellows of a turning-leaf filled autumn; and pink explosions of tacky love distance me from the vast and varied possibilities of a new year (while reminding me that, in terms of romance, I am lacking). If we refuse to buy Halloween candy until October 1st, if we wait to adorn our businesses and homes with trees and tinsel until after our Thanksgiving turkeys have been digested, if we scoff at the Valentine's hearts that beat prematurely in the wake of Santa's sleigh, might we be able to stop this practice? Might we be able to help ourselves?

A Drawing and Quartering of Doves

Each fall the struggle renews itself — trying to induce a new collection of self-conscious, unsure of themselves teenagers to open up, to pose questions, to offer observations. Once my inherent wisdom and rectitude has been firmly established in my students' minds, a process, I assure you, which does not take long, I continue urging them to be active and engaged participants in class. When they express fears of seeming stupid, I reach into my well-stocked arsenal of idiocy and share a tale or two to inspire a kinship of sorts. A favorite involves (in my early 30s, mind) a hot beverage and a hotel stay.

Some background. We docked in Catalina on Christmas Eve, two widows and their daughters on a quest to avoid tradition and being home for the holidays, hoping the new vacancies in our hearts would feel less profound in a foreign environment. We arrived at our hotel to find it locked and deserted. Phone calls did not help. Though far from Joseph and a divinely pregnant Mary, we felt connected to those bereft travelers; it seemed there was no room for us at the inn. Lodgings eventually secured without resorting to an obliging barn, four-legged beasts for bedfellows, we checked in, retiring to our respective rooms.

Omitting this sad preamble, I only divulge to the class that, in need of a cupful of comfort, I readied a mug of instant cocoa using the hot water tap. Tepid at best. The kitchen nook boasted a coffee pot, a mini fridge, and ahh! — a microwave. Drink settled on tray, I close the door, though the latch seems off somehow. I punch in numbers — two minutes should do it — and wait. Nothing happens. I key in the number again. Nothing. Ahh! — not a microwave. "Kids, this is the lady who attempted to heat her hot chocolate in the hotel safe. You're not gonna sound stupid!" If extra ammunition proves necessary, I am prepared; many more arrows fledged with imbecility dwell in that quiver. I might mention my childhood belief that the vacuum cleaner mowed the carpet, how I recall eyeing my mother as she once again worked her way around the house. Why so often? If the carpet had grown in the interim since the last cleaning, it can only have been infinitesimally.

But humans aren't the only error-prone entities. What mistakes do elephants make, I wonder. And daffodils and mountains? Technology flubs are something easier to identify. Voice to text comes to mind. A hand and arm given to loudly objecting when taxed with too much typing and mouse manipulation compelled its use and I applaud its invention though, considering I'm only referencing my right side, this applause remains rather less than impressive. While my whole self does appreciate the application, my editing self grows weary of fixing all the random capitalizations, the inability of the microphone to differentiate between my ins and ands, and the wild misinterpretations of certain words and phrases. Since the latter has been known to provoke exuberant laughter, I'm willing to forgive that flaw...to an extent. A favorite mishearing occurred when I began using the program for school. When speaking my professional name, Ms. Finstuen, voice to text could not grasp the moniker. Trying its feeble best, I noticed my signature appeared as one Misfits Doing. Of course I liked this so much I started using it in lieu of my identity (or does it understand me more accurately than I've given credit? I am, with considerable frequency, a misfit who is doing). Amusement is a constant visitor when reading over what I've just spoken to the screen, while its companion, Thank Goodness I Caught That Before Sending or Saving, often stops by to say hello. What could fall under both guises involves a quotation from *East of Eden*, a book I reread last summer. As is my habit, I type up notes and quotes I particularly wish to remember. Uttering Samuel's impassioned speech about the different translations of a certain passage in the Bible, I concluded my recitation, sitting back to read over the passage. Instead of "'Thou mayst!'" the screen showed: "'They'll mess, dumbass!'" Here again I perceive a certain uncanny depth of understanding. This is, after all, an accurate description of human nature, not to mention an innovative way to express the concept of original sin. Yes, we'll mess — all of us dumbasses.

Hear that, kids?

A Trampling of Emus

I've been thinking about the id bracelet trend of my childhood. If you are a) currently middle-aged or b) the parent of a middle-aged (I want to put "child" here — isn't that telling?) child, perhaps you remember those silver rectangles clasped about the developing wrists of the youngsters of the 1980s. Name, address, phone number. Essentially pet licenses for humans. When did they go out of fashion? I can't remember, though they all but vanished; is that a form of irony in that their very presence attempted to thwart disappearance?

In recent years I've imagined bringing them back, with one form of pertinent information substituting another. Instead of data, potentially hazardous personality traits would be etched into the metal. We're mostly walking Rorschach tests, consistently misinterpreted. With these adornments we could instantly ascertain that Casey embroiders the truth (liberally); Jonas always strays over the dividing line in parking lots *and* named his twins Patience and Temperance (now there's a recipe for impetuousness and dipsomania); Fiona is waaaayy too sensitive; Gregory is generally sweet, but ferociously competitive at Monopoly — even when volunteering at the retirement home; Dana doesn't understand the social norm regarding the proper time to leave a social gathering; Leslie is inadvertently caustic (and vertently manipulative); Wallace fishes for compliments with the seamy bait of self-deprecation. And Quentin? Well, he's just an asshole.

What would be emblazoned on your bracelet and what on mine? While I like to think "I am an excellent person whose moral compass should steer the ship of the respectable world" an apt summary, it wouldn't very well fit the bangle's intended purpose. Surely then, my antisocial tendencies would be listed at the top.

Social awkwardness must be the impetus for many a delightful anecdote — shameful too, when it comes to it, but let's leave those for another time. I wonder if others who do not thrive in communion develop tactics to stick in the conversational tool belt should their use and application prove necessary. One of my own involves preplanning topics to discuss or questions to ask should a rather too long pause linger between words.

An acquaintance from college — we cohered due to our similar plights: both beginning freshmen halfway through the year, neither of us Christian at a heavily conservative, Christian institution. He left after that first joint semester, but I remained, the supposed evil outsider, suspicious glances a part of my curriculum.

Nearly two years following the separation I received a call from Chad. He was to be in town and would I like to have lunch? I said yes before considering the reality of the discomfort likely to serve as a side dish of such a repast. Supplied with keys and wallet, I fastened that belt, poorly supplied perhaps, but still offering a sense of security and comfort.

We ate on a pleasant, petal-adorned patio, rambling the grounds of polite banter. A pause. A lengthening pause. I unsheathed a prepared question. I would be going to see the new Michelle Pfeiffer/Harrison Ford movie that evening and wondered if he had seen it. Just as the question rose to my lips, Chad — conceivably employing a ready-made string of words himself (i.e., in case of prolonged silence, offer the girl a compliment) — commented, "Katherine, I really like your skirt."

Before a reasonable thank you or my usual "I like it too" could be uttered, the canned question issued forth. "Have you seen *What Lies Beneath*?"

An even longer cessation than the previous one elapsed. He looked at me. I looked at him.

"Why nooooo." But has he seen the *movie*?

I do wonder had we first met arrayed in forewarning jewelry, would any attachment exist? Which is better? The immediate identification of attributes or their slow discovery through investment of time and contact? I think I know the answer but ask me again after Wallace corners me during intermission.

A Curse of Cardinals

Let us now turn our attention to the peculiar realm of city mottos. I can't claim to understand their existence, the majority being ridiculous, untrue, or simply unnecessary. But again, when there's a chance of amusement in *anything*, my appreciation expands like a boa constrictor upon swallowing a medium-sized mongoose. A few examples. My (not very impressive) history as a piano player began in third grade. My parents engaged a teacher (oh Mr. Evans, my memories of you are vast and varied!) who endured the "talents" of young musicians in a room above a music store located in the neighboring town. The weekly trip allowed me extra time with my father and a glimpse of the town's entrance sign "Welcome to Bothell...for a day or a lifetime." For us it was always a day, but given the shoddiness of my playing it often felt like a lifetime. My performance aside, who thought up that sparkling gem? Our own: "Woodinville — Country Living City Style" was even more inane and, given the resources available at the time, utterly fallacious. But Bothell's sign afforded the local pranksters a larger field for mischief. Every so often, entering the city limits we'd be bidden: "Welcome to hell...for a day or a lifetime." Again, given my lack of felicity with the ebony and ivory, Mr. Evans might describe my sojourn as just such a dip into perdition.

I have a strong affinity for another town in Washington due almost solely to its motto — a bumper sticker of which proclaims from my Prius: "It's an Edmonds kind of day!" Truthfully, I'm on my second sticker — a new vehicle merited a replacement, for one mustn't cease wishing one's brethren an Edmonds kind of day. I'm not exactly sure what this imparts though I did once contact the Chamber of Commerce seeking this information. Although I received a lengthy response in reply, I still can't attest to complete comprehension, though I'm assured it's a *good* thing. I did recently morph the motto into something rather less savory. Joking with a resident, a friend of my mother's (73 years of age but still blessed with the bawdiest of minds), I proposed she barhop (truly — she wears an orthopedic boot), flirting with the masculine youth given to forming quick assignations by proclaiming herself an Edmonds kind of lay. She's thinking about it.

But the best motto I've come across, and one that seems most closely linked to my own temperament, is that of Bellingham — The City of Subdued Excitement. What better way to express my reaction to most positive things in life? Bellingham gets itself and it clearly gets *me*. I think the majority of my family falls into the category of the subduedly excited, particularly my late father, a true paragon of the subdued dude. Had he been a town, the welcome sign would likely be etched with the words "Low Expectations" — his personal motto. Given his sense of humor, the board would likely sit atop an extremely short or entirely non-existent post, its own lowness causing it to escape all but those with the most astute vision. Such a shame for how many of us would benefit from pursuing life with a mantra characterized by diminished reward?

I've not yet fashioned a welcome sign of my own, though I may adopt Dad's — adding to the already accrued inheritance of his Dickens collection and a model viking boat. Still, certain by-laws are already in place. For example, when giving a compliment, don't use the word "actually" (just think about it). And please cease the practice of greeting others by asking "How are you?"

I pallbeared, if that is the verb for it, at my grandfather's funeral. I remember the shock of struggling with the weight of my portion of the coffin, being surrounded by my enormous brothers and cousins, all at the height of burly athleticism. It wasn't his death, no, that provoked discomfort of that query; this came with my father's, an unexpectedly few short years later. I've never thought it a good question — a social convention lacking anything of consequence. But in the stunned grief of Dad's disappearance, no, friendly grocery clerk and no, well-meaning receptionist, I really do not want to be asked how I am. I know humans tend to bristle at change, but now is the time for "How are you?" to quietly vacate such a centralized location in our lexicon. Its posure has grown even more distasteful as my own health has declined, as the health of the earth has declined, as the exposure of the true ugliness of our country has sickened us (or those of us with any sense of compassion or care, any dedication to justice and equality). Even with true friends it bothers, for with them, the information *will* come out through meaningful conversation in its own time. Yet another echo of a too common pleasantry is superfluous.

So half an orphan at 30, though the math doesn't figure exactly. The more years that pass, the more I notice him in me. Although he's been reduced to ashes and so many of his belongings have morphed into memory only, he is still more here than not. As to those belongings, a year after his death, my oldest brother and I sorted through his closet for our mother. She couldn't bear the smells, the sight of well-worn cardigans and faded jeans, extra wide shoes that supported his boxy feet, the robes and stoles (yes, my father was not only a father to us, but to many a Lutheran congregant).

At one point I emerged, a jar in my hand. "Is this Mt St. Helens?" I asked.

Mom looked at me, at the contents I gripped, before stating, "No. That's your dad." Part of him anyway — a portion rests sown into the folds of Mt. Rainier, another buried beneath a stone with his name and the dates of his birth and death. Her name and one of those dates already engraved next to the ominous blank space I can not bear to imagine filled. Part of him in this jar. Insubstantial. Loitering amidst unworn clothes (including, bizarrely, lederhosen he'd picked up on a college trip to Europe and which wouldn't fit very long after the purchase. Not fat, but definitely sturdy and yes, substantial). One more unanswered question for him. "Why lederhosen, Dad?"

Peter and I carted a load to the Goodwill (after trying on that article of clothing ourselves, of course). Just how many Goodwill finds are attributable to death, I wonder? I like to imagine some fat-footed lover of German paraphernalia romping about in this outfit, knowing in his heart the low expectations he had upon entering the store served only to enhance the subdued excitement kindled by this bargain.

Postlogue

At times the task of discarding the unused wafers and cheap wine (or body and blood of Christ if you're of the believing sort) following the Sunday service fell to me. Theologically speaking, they have been blessed; they are holy. One doesn't toss Christ upon the post-service coffee grounds. It can be hoped He continues to nourish the earth, is once again a participant in creation's glory. The church nestled itself in a declivity in what seemed to me at the time a vast forest. In tidy shoes and white ankle socks I'd follow the path into its depths. Cloaked in the subtle quiet of the fir tree canopy, I scattered the crumbs and poured the dregs, feeding Jesus to the birds in unique solitude before returning to the building, the throng, my family, and our journey home. To extend the metaphor while considering my own agnosticism (sorry, Dad), the reflections above, the arrangement of words into curious groupings are more accurately considered scraps to be pecked at by birds, that is, read by humans who, in their own collectives often form such communities as charms, but curses as well. We are wonderful; we are terrible. But in all our guises we still need never litter or fail to return our grocery carts to their designated lanes.

www.ingramcontent.com/pod-product-compliance
Lightning Source LLC
Chambersburg PA
CBHW042353070526
44585CB00028B/2919